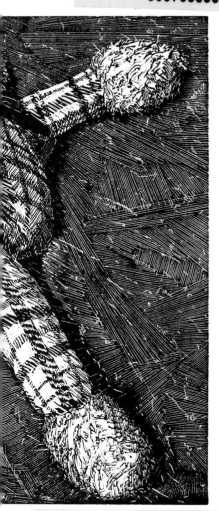

TEDDY BEARS

TEDDY BEARS

SUE PEARSON

SILENT BOOKS
CAMBRIDGE

ACKNOWLEDGEMENT

Thanks are due to the following people for their kind permission to reproduce the illustrations listed below.

Dottie Ayers for Front cover and pages 14, 21, 33, 40
Peter Smith for Endpapers and page 17
Lisa Chapman for pages 28, 44
Sarah Chamberlain for page 48
Our thanks also to:
Teddy: Simon Bond (Methuen, London); *Little Bear*: Maurice Sendak (Harper & Row, New York); *Teddy Bear Robinson*: Joan Robinson (Harrap Publishing Group Ltd); *Veterinary Record April 1st 1972*: Veterinary Record, London; *A Ring of Bells by John Betjeman*: Edward Ardizzone (John Murray Publishers Ltd); *The Golden Budget of Nursery Stories*: Frank Adams (Blackie and Son Ltd, Glasgow); *Blue Teddy and Pink Teddy*: John Astrop (Macdonald & Co. Publishers Ltd, London); *Berryman Cartoon*: (MacMillan Publishing Inc, New York).

Additional picture research by Godfrey and Jan Waller.

First published in Great Britain 1990
by Silent Books, Swavesey, Cambridge CB4 5RA

© Text copyright Sue Pearson 1990

ISBN 1 85183 024 3

Typeset by Goodfellow & Egan, Cambridge
Printed in Great Britain by Redwood Press Ltd, Melksham, Wiltshire

CONTENTS

To my Mother
who started me on the road to collecting
by giving me my first bear

INTRODUCTION

I collect old teddy bears because they have a special appeal for me. The fact that they have all been loved for so many years by different people, children and adults like, gives them great personality and charm. Old bears have comforted their owners when they have been ill or unhappy and been a friend and companion to them during the good times. All this has left the bears with wear and tear which only serves to make them more lovable.

I keep my bears at home sitting in old chairs and on old horses, in old prams and dolls' beds – anywhere they look nice and comfortable and happy – where I look at them and imagine the people who once owned and loved them.

I like to collect bears that have interesting stories to them; perhaps I have photographs or documentation about the people who owned them. These stories bring the bear's past to life and give a link with their owners. Sometimes their stories are sad. One of my bears belonged to a little boy who died in 1917; it was then given to his sister, who sold it to me when she was in her eighties. Other stories are romantic, such as that of the couple who married at the beginning of the century. He was a colonel in the army and his wife always called him her 'big bear'. He was a very tall man and she was very small and so before he was posted to Africa he bought her a bear which they called 'little bear'. He died and was buried in Africa and she kept 'little bear' with her for the rest of her life. Now 'little bear' lives with me and gives me much pleasure. No wonder these old bears have a special aura about them.

Many of my old bears in the first half of this century belonged to families who were in the colonial service and so they travelled to Africa, India and all the far-flung countries of the Empire. Some of these bears have coats or little suits that were sewn by their Indian or Chinese servants, perhaps to protect their mohair when going a bit thin.

My bears come out with me when I go to lecture on old bears. They have a lovely time because when I have finished talking I let my audience come and have a closer look. The bears are really spoilt, being given lots of cuddles. I hear comments like 'Aren't they beautiful?', and 'He's handsome', and there are many 'oohs' and 'ahs' of appreciation. In this way they continue to give pleasure to a lot of people, receiving a lot of love in return.

My first old bear I had as a child had belonged to my mother, who had been given him in 1910. He had been her favourite toy and then he was passed on to me. He came in remarkably good condition. He is straw-filled, with black

DOTTIE AYERS

D. Ayers

· 14 ·

shoe-button eyes and wearing a pin-striped waistcoat, with silver buttons, tailored by my grandmother. He has always sat on a chair in my bedroom except for an interval after we had moved house when he went missing. I searched high and low for him but I could not find him. However I never gave up hope. One day my daughter was looking through an old tin trunk in the attic when, lo and behold, there was my bear. We were reunited and he is back on his chair in my bedroom.

I have been very fortunate in having old dolls and toys around me since I was very young. My parents were great

HONOR C APPLETON

HCA

collectors of antiques and when they were buying furniture
and porcelain for themselves they would often buy me an
old doll or toy. In those days they were comparatively cheap
because there was not the level of interest there is today. I
am very grateful to my parents for giving me an interest in
old things.

I started dealing in dolls and bears about 15 years ago, at first in an antique market; however, it had always been my dream to have my own shop, so when four years ago a very pretty little shop in the conservation area of Brighton came on the market, I bought it. Since then I have gradually filled it with the things I love, old dolls and teddy bears, dolls' prams and cots, teddy bear-related items such as postcards, china, bears in carved wood and miniature furniture for bears to sit on.

I have people come to see me from all over England and indeed the world, so my teddies go off on their travels again with their delighted new owners.

THE HISTORY OF THE TEDDY BEAR

First of all let me clear up one myth about the teddy bear: there is no such thing as a Victorian teddy bear. Teddy bears were born in the early part of this century and certainly not in Victorian days.

The Origin of the Name

Why is the bear called 'Teddy'? The first Teddy was Theodore Roosevelt, who became President of the United States of America in 1901. In 1902 the President went on a hunting trip to the state of Mississippi. After several days with no success his hosts became desperate and found a poor little bear cub which they tied to a tree and invited him to shoot. The President thought this was most unsporting and refused, and so he went home empty-handed. Clifford Berryman, a political cartoonist on the Washington *Evening Star*, portrayed this event in a cartoon showing the President in a good light, making Teddy and his bear famous.

Soon after this the first bears, which were called Bruin, appeared as table decorations at the wedding reception of Theodore Roosevelt's daughter Alice. They were dressed as sportsmen and one of the President's guests asked her jokingly, 'What breed of bear are these?' 'Why, Teddy's bears of course,' she replied. This story was carried in the American newspapers and 'Teddy's bears' soon became famous all over the country.

BIRTH OF THE TEDDY BEAR (1902)
The tubby cub supplanted wooly lambs.

The First Teddy Bears

At that time, Morris Michtom, originally from Russia where there is a great tradition of bears, saw the cartoon in the Washington *Evening Star*. He and his wife had a little retail store selling candies and toys. They sent a sample of a toy bear, which they designed from the picture, to President

Roosevelt asking him if he would lend his name to this toy. Legend has it that Teddy Roosevelt wrote back saying that he did not think his name was worth much but they were welcome to use it if they wished. Morris Michtom and his wife produced many teddy bears; they became the Ideal Toy Corporation of America and made some very attractive bears.

Also at about that time Margarete Steiff in a small town in Germany was making her first Bruins. These were sold at the Leipzig fair of 1903 to a buyer for a large American import house who imported them to the USA, where they became an immediate hit.

Which one, Steiff or Michtom, came first is not certain. There is so much legend woven round the origins of the teddy bear that it all makes a very charming story.

The German Steiff Bears

The early Steiff bears are the most sought-after teddy bears and also the most difficult to find.

Margarete Steiff had a nephew called Richard who studied sculpture at the Stuttgart School of Arts and Craft, and in his spare time he spent many hours sketching the performing bears at the circus. From these sketches came the first bear toy with movable joints, which became immediately very popular. Before the first world war the Germans dominated the market with their bears; 1907 was called the year of the bear, and they sold thousands of bears in that year. Margarete Steiff died in 1909 but her motto 'only the best is good enough for our children', lived on. The Steiff factory is still producing bears today.

D. Ayers

Early English Bears

The English toy manufacturers were not far behind the Steiff bears. One of the early ones was J.K. Farnell.

Farnell bears were sold at Harrods, London, and it was from there that Christopher Robin Milne was bought a bear for his first birthday in 1921. The original Farnell bear was called Edward. Christopher Robin's Edward became Winnie the Pooh, and he is now on display in America.

Farnell are lovely bears to collect. They were made with very fine quality Yorkshire cloth, a thick golden mohair which has survived well. They are very chubby, quite wide round the middle – Winnie the Pooh was often in trouble for his weight.

YOUR FIRST TEDDY BEAR

Learning all the different names and makes of teddy bears can be very difficult because unfortunately teddies do not always come with stamps and marks on them like silver, porcelain or antique dolls. Books are invaluable for reference, and I do strongly recommend you to use them, but nothing actually beats handling bears, picking them up, talking to people, and asking about them.

If you are new to collecting, go to a reputable dealer to buy your first teddy bear. You will generally find dealers

HONOR C APPLETON

very glad to share their knowledge with you and they will show you all the different types of bears. Do be careful of buying a bear from somewhere you do not have confidence in. There are imitations and forgeries. Bears may be made from old fabric to look like old ones, they are distressed, their paws are torn, but they are not old. You can pay a large sum of money for one of these bears and it is very sad when you discover you do not have the real thing.

Choosing your Teddy Bear

People often ask my advice about what to look for when buying a bear. The first and most important point when you are choosing a bear is that he should speak to you. Look at his face and his size and his expression and think 'I really want that bear. That bear's for me. It's a special bear.' The second point is that you should be able to afford him. Try to keep within your price range, though this can be difficult sometimes. Often it is not the cost of the bear that is important. I have got many teddy bears at home that have lost an arm or an eye but still I love them. The aim is to

How nicely they have their dinner.

collect within your price range and to find various types of bear – English, American, German – from very early bears right up until the 1950s. I stop there because I only collect bears that are pure wool or mohair, I do not have any bears that are made of synthetic fabric. These old bears are stuffed either with straw, straw and kapok, or kapok. They are the most desirable bears.

The Value of a Teddy Bear

The value of teddy bears depends very much on their age and condition; obviously the early bears are always more expensive. It is very difficult to find a bear with a complete furry coat, most of them have bald patches and thin areas. When you do find one in very good condition, he can often be two or three times the price of the same bear in poor condition. However, as long as you pay the right price for the right type of bear it does not matter too much if he is bald, provided you like him. I have many bears in my collection that have an arm or a leg which has been patched, but I love them just the same.

Be careful about buying a bear that is rotten and brittle. Any bear in this condition can only get worse. As you try to stitch them, the fabric crumbles away. However, old bears often have replaced pads, which is quite acceptable.

The advice of a good dealer is essential to guide you to the right price for a particular bear.

The illustration shows H.E.S. Pricey, so named because the old general dealer who had him at the back of his shop scratched his head when asked how much he was and said, 'Oh him! I'm afraid he's pricey, madam.'

He is my king bear and he usually sits in an old child's high chair at the top of our stairs. He is a very eccentric bear and at one time looked so fierce that he had his mouth remodelled so that now he has a slightly lopsided smile.

Bears with Their Original Labels

Many bears would have had tags or labels, but over the years many of them have been lost. If you do find a bear with this label that you like and can afford, I think it is a good buy, in this way gradually building up your collection with examples of all the different manufacturers – Steiff, Farnell, Chad Valley, Merrythought and Deans being the most important – getting to know each one's characteristics. Certainly any bear with a label is always worth more, if it is in good condition, than a bear without a label.

Many of the early bears had buttons in their ears or on their sides which have been taken off by children, so any of those with their little buttons still on are particularly collectable.

LISA CHAPMAN

CARE OF YOUR TEDDY BEARS

Do ask advice on looking after your teddy bear. Your dealer is the best person to advise you on the care of the bear you have just bought from him.

Care of Your Newly Acquired Bear

Having brought your newly acquired teddy bear home, if he has already been cleaned and restored you can introduce him to his new bear friends immediately.

However, if you have bought him from a jumble sale or a market and he is dirty, you must keep him in isolation for two weeks until you are sure he does not have any moths or other insects on him which he could pass on to your other bears. One of the best ways to do this is to seal him in a plastic bag with some mothballs. Alternatively, put him in the deep freeze sealed tightly in a plastic bag for one week.

When I am certain there are no insects, I always clean my bears, because dirt can rot fabric and attract moths. Because they are made of pure wool mohair they clean up very well. First I inspect them carefully and give them a brush or, if possible, use a small hand-held vacuum with some net or cheesecloth over the nozzle secured with an elastic band. Vacuum or brush your bear thoroughly to remove any dust and loose dirt.

General Care

I brush my teddy bears this way every 2 to 3 weeks to make

sure there is no moth damage. I usually keep some lavender bags or cedar blocks near my teddy bears to deter moths from spoiling them.

It is very important for old bears to be kept away from direct sunlight because any sunlight is bad for old fabric, causing it to rot and fade. Many teddy bears have different colours on them from being exposed to sunlight, they may be faded on one side with their original colour on the other.

Cleaning Old Teddy Bears

It is possible to clean teddy bears but I do recommend that you take professional advice. I have actually bought teddy bears out of attics where they have been lying uncovered,

RUB-A-DUB-DUB, TEDDY BEAR'S IN THE TUB.

face down. One side has been completely coated with dust and grime while the other side was as new. After I have cleaned them very, very carefully they are all one colour again, but it does take a great deal of patience and skill.

A word of advice; never put an old bear in a washing machine or spin dryer. They hate it and usually never recover from it. It is surprising how many bears I have had brought into my shop that have received such treatment.

The technique is to use a special liquid soap, 'woolite', available from most supermarkets, with cold water and whisk it to get a good foam. I work the foam into the bear from the head down using a soft sponge. Do not get the fabric wet. Clean only the mohair and then leave the teddy bear to sit for ten minutes while you get a bowl of warm water and a clean dishcloth. Wring it out in the water and with a circular motion remove the foam from the bear, changing the water and rinsing the dishcloth often. Repeat this several times as you do not want to leave any foam in the mohair. Get a towel and dry your bear. Then take a fine comb and gently comb out the mohair. Leave him to dry completely for 48 hours. You will be surprised at how nice he looks, and you will have a very happy bear.

If you are in any doubt, it is better to have your bear professionally cleaned than risk damaging him through poor cleaning. Your dealer will be able to advise you on a suitable person to do this for you.

Repairing Old Bears

When bears are a bit thin or bald I put a dress or sweater or a knitted pullover on them – Grandmas are very good at knitting pullovers for threadbare bears. Sometimes if a bear has only one ear it is possible to use that ear to make two by dividing it and putting a backing on both pieces. Even if the bear, like one of mine, has only got one arm it is possible to make another arm and then put on a knitted sweater so that you cannot see the replaced limb.

If you ever need to repad a bear that has very passé hands but still has its original label, remove the label very carefully, put a new pad on the teddy bear and then sew the label over the new pad.

When you are looking for a teddy bear, all that I have said about repairs does depend on the price. If you think the price is right when you see a bear which needs some repairs, and you love him and can afford him, then go ahead and buy him.

Storage of your Teddy Bears

Teddy bears like to join in with family things, sitting in the lounge or on your landing or in your bedroom, being with people. Most of them have spent their lives being somebody's best friend and companion, so when they come into your collection they will still want to be that.

However, sometimes it is necessary to put away your teddy bears. Please, please do not put them into plastic bags. Teddy bears cannot breathe in plastic, which makes their natural fabric sweat and causes them to rot. The way to store your teddy bears is to wrap them in acid-free tissue and put them in cardboard boxes in a dry airy place, nowhere damp.

JOHN ASTROP

The following is an extract from 'Some observations on the diseases of *Brunus edwardii* (species nova) by D.K. Blackmore BSc, PhD, FRCVS, D.G. Owen MSc and C.M. Young MA, Vet MB, MRCVS, published in the *Veterinary Record* on 1 April 1972.

'Examination Technique

Examinations were carried out as quickly as possible, because many owners were reluctant to be parted from their bears for long. No restraint was necessary, as the bears showed no apprehension and were obviously used to being handled. An attempt was made to record body temperature, but this was abandoned, as all specimens appeared to be homoiothermic. Each bear was given a thorough external examination, and data were collected on approximate age, weight, condition and colour of coat and physical disabilities. Stuffing condition was assessed by careful palpation. Where necessary, radiographs were taken, and biopsies obtained to

identify the stuffing material. Subcutaneous and deeper tissues often protruded from superficial abrasions and, where necessary, a small seam incision was made, a sample taken, and the opening sutured with Coats Machine Twist 30, using a standard Milwards darning needle. Voice boxes, where present, were tested by percussion and auscultation.

The psychological state of the bear was assessed by examining the facial expression, and also by investigating the case history with special reference to the frequency and duration of association with children.

Case 1

A 10-year-old bear, which had been owned successively by three siblings. The normal yellow coat colour had changed to a dirty grey, there was extensive alopecia which had progressed to 'threadbearness' over the ears, nose and limb extremities. The axillary and inguinal seams were weak, resulting in intermittent dislocation of the limbs, but there was no herniation of stuffing. Old age, and persistent handling with transport by one limb were the main reasons for the chronic debility, for which there is no satisfactory treatment.

Case 2

A 16-year-old bear, with an asymmetrical expression and obvious emotional disturbance, found at the back of a cupboard. After the removal of superficial dust, the coat condition was seen to be good, but the animal had a permanent squint, due to careless replacement of the right eye with a shoe button. Tracing the case history revealed that this bear had suffered recurrent unilateral ocular prolapse, which had progressed to total rupture of the filamentous orbital attachments, and loss of the eye. It was hoped that a new owner might be found for this animal, and that with a newly matched pair of eyes his expression and psychological state might improve.

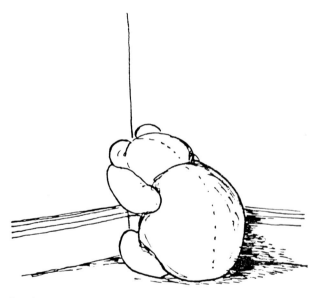

Case 3

An aged, cobweb-covered bear, found in an attic. Its general condition was poor, with loss of a forelimb, and herniation of stuffing. The frontal seam was ruptured, exposing a rusted voice box with helical weakness. The animal was heavily infested with commensals, which included a pair of *Mus musculus* with two generations of young, a total of 23 individuals. Specimens of *Laelaps hilaris, Leptosylla segnis, Nosopsyllus fasciatus* and *Lepisma saccharina* were found in the right inguinal region, and the border of the left pinna was being eroded by clothes moths (*Tineola bisselliella*). Treatment of this case included vigorous shaking, dusting with pyrethrum, a stuffing transfusion, and a forelimb graft.'

MAJOR TEDDY BEAR
MANUFACTURERS

Steiff Bears

Steiff bears have distinguished looks and high-quality workmanship. The early bears are easily recognisable by their very long arms and curving paws; their arms reach right down to their ankles when they sit up and they have a very distinctive hump. Their faces have black button eyes and extra long noses embroidered with black thread, they

DOTTIE AYERS

have slim long feet with felt pads also embroidered with black thread. They are stuffed with a wood wool and had growlers which made the bear growl when he was tipped back and forth. Sadly many of these do not work today, but that in no way affects their value. Sometimes when an old bear is restored, the growler is still inside him.

Margarete Steiff established the famous *Knopf im Ohr* (button in the ear) trademark in 1905 to stop her designs being pirated. This is a small metal button that fixed to the ear which can be right down inside making it quite difficult to find. Not all Steiff bears still have this button because over the years they have been removed by parents and children alike. The early buttons are of pewter colour and quite small. Beware that somebody has not put a modern Steiff button in an old bear's ear to try to make him look like an old Steiff.

Chiltern Bears

One of my favourite types of bear was made by an English firm called Chiltern; these are very popular with today's collectors.

The brand name for Chiltern Toys was registered in 1924 by H.G. Stone and Leon Rees, who had become partners and acquired the Chiltern factory in Chesham, Buckinghamshire. They continued producing toys there until the company was bought by Chad Valley in 1967.

These bears have a label sewn to the seam on the side of the body which reads 'Chiltern Hygienic Toys, Made in England'. They have very appealing faces often with a black plastic nose which combined with whiskery mohair on their faces gives them a slightly doggy look. I believe that the plastic nose was actually used on their toy dogs until one day somebody thought of putting it on a bear. It certainly gives them a distinctive look.

Chiltern bears are a typically English shape, with a wide head and short nose, and being rather plump bears they are very cuddly. Their stuffing is kapok and they often have velvet pads on long narrow feet. They range in size from very large right down to quite tiny, all of which make an attractive addition to any collection.

Chad Valley Bears

During the first world war imports of toys from Germany were stopped, giving English toy manufacturers the opportunity to fill the gap this created in the market. Toy companies were soon expanding, helped by the fact that England was a major producer of the cloth needed to make bears and soft toys. One of these was a firm called Chad Valley, established in 1920. They produced the famous Bonzo the dog and also a large range of felt dolls.

Their bears are really delightful, often with a label sewn to the foot making them easy to identify. Before the 1930s they used the words 'Hygienic Toys, Made in England by the Chad Valley Co. Ltd.' After 1938, when Chad Valley was given a royal appointment, the label read 'The Chad Valley Co. Ltd. by Appointment Toymakers to H.M. Queen Elizabeth' [now, of course, the Queen Mother] and displayed a royal crest. Like Steiff bears, they also had metal buttons in their ears with 'Chad Valley English Hygienic Toys' on them.

Chad Valley are typically English bears, made in mohair with a wide head and short nose with wide stitching.

In 1978 the firm was taken over by an American company and all their old catalogues were destroyed, much to the frustration of anyone wanting to find out more about these charming bears.

LITERARY BEARS

Early Teddy Bear Stories

Perhaps the earliest teddy bear story of all is of Goldilocks and the three bears, a traditional story, possibly from Russia, which has passed into the folklore of storytelling worldwide. The illustration by Frank Adams shows the three bears looking very much like the early Bruins.

Some of the first stories about teddy bears were written in America between 1906 and 1910 by Seymour Eaton, also known as Paul Piper, and illustrated by Floyd Campbell. He wrote about the Roosevelt Bears, Teddy G (Good) and

FRANK ADAMS

THE THREE BEARS

"Someone has been tasting my porridge!"

SARAH CHAMBERLAIN

· 48 ·

Teddy B (Bad), and their great adventures on their travels round America and the world. They were very popular when first published; however, these stories are now long out of print.

One of the earliest British teddy bear stories was about Rupert, who is still very popular today. Mary Tourtel, the wife of a Daily Express sub-editor, first created him in 1916,

and he has appeared in the *Daily Express* almost every day since. Alfred Bestall, a Fellow of the Royal Academy, took over Rupert in 1935 when Mary Tourtel was unable to continue working. Mary Tourtel also created Nutwood, where Rupert lives with Bill Badger, Algy Pug and Edward Trunk. These characters all appear in children's annuals, and other story books where Rupert is always seen in his idiosyncratic red jersey and checked trousers with his yellow scarf, and gum boots to complete his outfit.

The Illustrators

As teddy bears became more popular, more stories were written about them, some were for very young children as

MAURICE SENDAK

EDWARD ARDIZZONE

simple board books, as alphabet books to help them learn the alphabet, and as colouring books. Soon teddy bears were used as the basis for stories for children of all ages.

Almost every children's story about teddy bears has been illustrated, and it is the quality of these illustrations which has often determined the lasting success of any particular story. Some illustrators were famous in other fields such as Maurice Sendak, illustrator of *Where the Wild Things are* and

Edward Ardizzone, who illustrated over 200 books. Some became well known through their work on teddy bears, notably E.H. Shepard for his exquisite Winnie the Pooh illustrations.

Sadly some illustrators' delightful work has slipped away

as the books have gone out of print because the storyline has become dated. The illustrations of Honor Appleton in Mrs H.C. Cradock's book *The Best Teddy Bear in the World* fall into this category.

For Adults Only

Teddy bears are not confined solely to children's books; they are also found in literature. One of the best-known is Aloysius in Evelyn Waugh's memorable novel, *Brideshead Revisited*. Sir John Betjeman, a contemporary undergraduate of Evelyn Waugh at Oxford University, had a much-loved bear called Archibald Ormsby-Gore who is mentioned

in the poem, 'Summoned By Bells', and in a short story entitled *Archie and the Strict Baptists*. These two bears were treated with great respect by their authors, but Simon Bond, author of *A Hundred and One Uses of a Dead Cat*, in his book, *Teddy*, takes a much more irreverent look at the place of teddy bears in society and our hearts, using cartoons to make penetrating comments on the human condition.

The Settings

Most stories and teddy bears are based on the home. Teddy Robinson, created by Joan G. Robinson, has lots of adventures with Deborah about everyday things that happen in and around her home.

However, Margaret J. Baker used a shoe shop as the background for her stories of the Shoe Shop Bears, Wellington Boots, Slippers and Socks. They lived most of their working lives in the shoe shop in Cordwainers' Row where they were kept to amuse young children who came in for shoes.

JOAN G. ROBINSON

A Happy Christmas

Little one, I wish for you
Happiness and sweet content,
And may this Christmas be for you
The happiest you have spent.

Winnie the Pooh

Arguably the most famous literary bear of all is Winnie the Pooh by A.A. Milne, illustrated by E.H. Shepard. Winnie the Pooh was first published on 14 October 1926 and the stories about him and his friends, Kanga, Tigger and Eeyore, were very popular during the late 1920s and the 1930s, and this popularity continues to grow today.

Through Winnie the Pooh A.A. Milne created a poignant world of childhood which adults can identify with, and as they read the stories to their children perhaps Winnie the Pooh speaks as much to them as to their children, evoking memories of their own childhood, striking a chord of softness in the everyday adult routine.

FURTHER READING

Teddy Bears Past and Present: A Collector's Identification Guide. Linda Mullins. Hobby House Press, 900 Frederick Street, Cumberland, MD 21502, USA. 1987.

Periodicals
The UK Teddy Bear Guide. Hugglets, PO Box 290, Brighton, East Sussex, BN2 1DR, UK. Published annually.

The Teddy Bear and Friends, Hobby House Press. Published 6 times a year.

PLACES OF INTEREST

United Kingdom
Sue Pearson, 131/2 Prince Albert Road, Brighton, East Sussex, BN1 1HE. Telephone: 0273 29247.

London Toy and Model Museum, 23 Craven Hill, London, W2 3EN. Telephone: 071 262 7905. Paddington Bear archive.

Teddy Bear Museum, 19 Greenhill Street, Stratford upon Avon, Warwickshire, CV37 6LF. Telephone: 0789 293160.

Judy Sparrow's Bear Museum, 38 Dragon Street, Petersfield, Hampshire, GU31 4JJ. Telephone: 0730 65108. A private collection open to the public, restorations undertaken.

Museum of Childhood, 42 High Street, Edinburgh EH1 1TG. Telephone: 031 225 2424, ext. 6645.

Germany
The Steiff Museum, Giengen an der Brenz, Baden-Wurttemberg, D 7928. Telephone: 7322 1311. Seconds for sale in the shop.

United States of America
Smithsonian, Washington, D.C.

Margaret Woodbury Strong Museum, 700 Allen Creek Road, Rochester, New York 14618.

THE END